Bosque Redondo:
The Encircled Grove

Other Books
by Keith Wilson

Sketches For A New Mexico Hill Town

II Sequences

The Old Car

Graves Registry & Other Poems

Homestead

Rocks

The Shadow of Our Bones

The Old Man & Others: Some Faces for America

Psalms for Various Voices

Midwatch

THANTOG: Song s of a Jaguar Priest

The Shaman Deer

While Dancing Feet Shatter The Earth

Desert Cenote

The Streets Of San Miguel

Retablos

Stone Roses: Poems From Transylvania

Lovesongs & Mandalas

Meeting At Jal

Lion's Gate: Selected Poems

The Winds Of The Pentecost

Graves Registry

The Way Of The Dove

Warrior Song & Other Poems

Bosque Redondo:

The Encircled Grove
New and Selected Poems

Keith Wilson

Poems by Keith Wilson

2/18/01   *KW*

Introduction by Rudolfo Anaya

Typesetting: Katherine Forrest
Typeface is Caslon & Americana Extrabold

Cover Art: Rinconada Circa 1927, Victor Higgins (1884–1949).
Courtesy of Zaplin-Lampert Gallery, Santa Fe.

Library of Congress Card Catalog Number: 97-075995
Publisher: Pennywhistle Press

ISBN: 0-938631-35-7 paper

First Edition 2000

Acknowledgements:
Thanks to Cloudline, Contact II, Coyote's Journal, Bluefish, Blue Mesa Review, Floating Island, Gila Valley Review, Hudson Review, Kayak, Limberlost Review, Longhouse, Southwest Heritage, Stone Drum, Sumac, Tarasque, Transition, Western American Poetry, and Whole Notes. The "Selected Poems" were first published by Grove Press, Kayak Press, The University Press, Utah State University. Some of these poems were also reprinted in Lion's Gate: Selected Poems by Cinco Puntos Press with copyright permissions from the above presses.

Dedicated to

Grandfather,

Heloise,

& Gerry Abear

Contents

Note: ●◆ this mark indicates the poem continues on the following page.

INTRODUCTION

Bosque Redondo is a moving collection of poems whose theme is the evocative power of memory. In the hands of the poet memory becomes the catharsis that opens up the world of childhood, a space the poet must revisit. It is this power to evoke and bring to life a world of fabulous characters and the spirit of the place that makes Keith Wilson the master poet he is.

In these poems we visit the Río Pecos, river of Keith's childhood, and we meet the elders who influenced the poet. People and place are what we honor in our land, and by bringing the people of his childhood to life Keith honors that memory, as painful as it may be. The people portrayed are authentic, honest, disturbing, wise and foolish, sometimes tortured, but they always emit a glint of hope.

The elders of the Río Pecos walk through these pages. The people who swept around his childhood are celebrated, but Keith also brings to life the place, the Fort Sumner region. The world of the Pecos River and the eastern llano of New Mexico is after all the crucible of his poetic passion. The place is of primary importance for the child who lived through the harsh, turbulent, and sometimes redeeming times that were the 1940s in New Mexico.

Keith learned to read the signs of the land, for the land is full of symbols. The snake that appears in the poems informs us of the creative energy of the place. Keith has harnessed that energy in his poetry, and in doing so he transcends place to tell stories about the pain and joy of life. For that we thank him.

—*Rudolfo Anaya*

Bosque Redondo

is a Spanish term meaning roughly "a rounded or encircled wood, a grove of trees" and is the earlier name for a large cluster of cottonwoods and salt cedars along a bend in the Pecos River of New Mexico. The Comanche name for the place is now lost. Bosque Redondo is southeast of the present village of Fort Sumner, right alongside the Llano Estacado or Staked Plain, stretching from the Sangre de Cristo, Blood of Christ, Mountains to Corpus Christi, Body of Christ, Texas (itself an Indian word).

It was there, in that Valley, with its legends, that my father's friend, his compadre, died on the cross one Easter morning and my father's grief and loss spun him off into a lifetime of alcoholism. It was also where my greatuncle Herbert Mead Valentine, loser of three fortunes died penniless and drunk on our living room floor. Grandmother watching over her strange brood even after her death; mother holding to her husband and her family, never let go. Uncle Keith Edwards, my godfather and the most important and loved man in my life continually saved us from the consequences of Daddy's long binges. My sister Marjorie and I watching in suspicious wonder the dramas that were played out in the House of Whispers, where little could be held to be true, or separated from the illusions, the magic that concealed the truth.

•◇

I grew up beside that haunted plain, among those haunted words, in the deep green valley of the Bosque. My grandfather homesteaded near the ranch headquarters for the old Maxwell-Abreau Grant and close to where the Apaches and Navajos had been forcefully and brutally relocated by Kit Carson after the Long Walk in the late 1880's. Many of the irrigation ditches were first dug by Indian hands while the United States Army tried to make farmers out of warriors Most of them died, men, women and children. To this day the name Bosque Redondo has a terrible history. But vicious people did those terrible things, not the land. Holy Mother Earth remains holy.

Billy the Kid was killed, they say, near my grandfather's house and his ghost and those of the Indians are believed by some to still walk the Valley. This book, however, is about my own ghosts, the fictions of my mind as I look behind me to find those dead still walking and talking about their lives, their land. They are all about me, surround me as I write this book.

River Girl

—for my wife Heloise
more precious is the touch
of your mouth in the shadow
—Borges

and I remember the shade
of cottonwoods, the deep green solitude.
Cedar breaks, with wind.

How you never stood beside me
there, where shadows became dreams:
sunlight, a confusion, a breaking of mirrors.

Wherever we are now, in the turnings
of nightmare, our worlds speeding us on
to separate destinies (though together)

we still walk that whispering River back
to our young faces enshrouded by trees, and green.
I have always held your eyes.
You cannot have them back now.

Los Penitentes, hermanos

de la luz,

Hermanos de sangre. Out of a New Mexican night a memory that
has haunted me all my life
penitentes, marching
singing, their torches
high arc against
the crest of the Hill

Sensing my mother, her fear, I holding her hand, 4, knowing
nothing of the needs of men—

backs raw from cactus whips
yet singing of light, they were
truly Brothers of the Light, brown men

chanting

—little Christs, singing
to the agonies, of the wounds
of the dying Cristo who led them bearing their sins with his own

it is His blood dripping
from that sky 64 years ago
that calls them forth singing now

they, climbing the high Hill
with Him, His neck bowed under
His cross, they light His way

torches, smoking and flaming
above the tall grass, after all
these years it is the
darkness they left behind.

Pecos Valley Poem

It was a different world then,
I tell my children, as men have
always done. There were two hotels
—The Commercial and the Rio Pecos—
over there. Your great grandfather
carried people and baggage in his wagon
from the train station down there
up to the hotels and the people
were fed and given rooms and in
the evenings used to sit out on
big porches and stare at customers
of the other hotel next door.

Or maybe they'd walk down to
the drugstore and have a coke
or walk across the street and look
into the window of the dry goods
store or the grocery. It was really
quiet at night. You can't imagine
how still everything became. Lights
out at seven for most people, not
much electricity in the homes, no
body on the road that led off across
the mesa to magical places with
unfamiliar names

●◆

One evening
a bunch of people were listening
to election results on the drug
store radio and two headlights
like puma eyes appeared out of
the Llano's darkness and one man said,
"Now would you just look at that!
Some damn fool out there on the road,
and after dark too!" That's the way
it was in those small villages
along the Pecos, those days.

THE HOMESTEAD TRIO
Homestead: Carpenter's House

A green frame house, trimmed
in white, falling down.
A memory of ice tea
served frosted in tall glasses,
of coal oil lamps yellow light
against old glass windows

—crickets, wind
in the salt cedars, New
Mexico in the '30's
where people lived
for evening & our
old men sat smoking
an hour away

—the darkness, Billy
the Kid's ghost walking
the long road from Pete
Maxwell's house to the Military
Cemetery, alone.

His slender gun with the
birds-head grip, his
effeminate laugh . . . .
the shadows.
Old Spanish people who
knew him, stayed off the
road at night, told
these stories of a destroyed
world while all fell
down around them.

Small town. A happiness
for children in old stories,
dreaming guns & battles,
bullets that never hurt.
Scalping that somehow
left hair intact.

Homestead. It's uncured
wood rotted in the earth
until at last it broke
of its own weight, split,
exposing the stained years
of the living and the dead.

The Carpenter
—for Herbert Mead Valentine

odor of
tobacco

latakia
perique

oil

(at some point
what surrounds
a man

becomes him
birds curl into form
the sharp air
is bright
with their woodchip smell
My granduncle
his long hands stroke
a hurtling plane

& dreams
shape themselves
from fragrant wood

cedar

oak

rich walnut

his hands, knobbed & grained
make cabinets rise
gleam in the oiled light.

The Carpenter's Wife: Rose

—For Rose Valentine

who as a young girl
hid in a wrinkled skin.

I saw her peeping out
of dry blue eyes, caught
a scent of lavender sachet,
dusty lace: her true ways
hidden behind golden glasses.

In her hands she remained
swift, gentle.

Sadness surrounds her.
Leaves, that as years,
curled, fell gracefully,
curved past shyness &
her youth shone out in flowers
in songs hummed while her
stiff fingers repaired
the wreckage brought daily
to her house, turning
in dust, spun past memories

her eyes take
in love a form
both comely & caressed

—as a singing bird, she arises
walks, aged bones left easily behind.

Pascola

When I was a young man I knew a very old man by the name of Pascola, which in Yaqui means, curiously enough, "old man." It's been years now since I thought of him or recalled his strangely withered and pinched old face, rather like a carved coconut or an old clay mask, with just wisps of dirty grey hair. Little tufts of it sprouted from each ear and each nostril. He had few teeth and when he smiled he tried to hide his mouth with this thin hand bobbing and dancing below his cunning eyes. Odd that I could for a moment forget him.

He sold tamales. Especially when the wind was cold and bit through my leather fur-trimmed coat and when especially I would turn one particular corner by the department store on my way home to alcoholism and silence, the wind would smash into me with an anger and a chill—almost as if it were waiting there in ambush for me—and I would see him, smell the gusts of rich aroma from his corn-wrapped, steaming tamales. And I would grow angry with him. I still can't believe that. Annoyed by that harmless old man, so eager to please even me, a boy of the Anglos who ruled the town,

but he stood there, trying not to sway, even to stagger under the blows of the same wind that assaulted me. I usually stopped. I remember that gratefully, and I talked to him. I spoke more Spanish then, and he always seemed pleased even though I never had the dime he charged for three tamales. When I received my allowance I would try to remember to save back at least one dime to put into his hand as I would say, "Por favor, Pascola, dame un tamal?" I can hear my voice saying those words I never said, feel that wind tearing at the cornhusks and blowing down that empty street where he still stands, his cold hands shadowing his dark mouth, his bright Indian eyes laughing at the future he must have seen standing behind me.

"Where There Is Water"*

*Place is your honor
as it is your wisdom.*
—Eudora Welty

But what could be made
of a place like this? I used
to ask. Such a small gash
on the face of spinning rock,
tiny to stars . . . .

a patch of green and brown
bright glint of the Pecos River
surrounded by sand and rock—
miles, miles of scrub brush.

How then does it hold me so
in my heart that I can go
away and yet hear clearly
the wind through the leaves
of its history so sharply
it slices the years away?

*Indian meaning of "pecos"

River Scenes

—for Joe Somoza

i

All rivers are highways to the mind.
That this one, Pecos, place of water,
was dry most of the year was no obstacle
to the dreams it could hold, pathway
that leads from where ever one wishes
not to be. The crows, the rabbits
snakes and mockingbirds become audience
as the fantasies of boyhood play
in theaters of tree and brush, wind
tugging at the hair, eyes half closed.

ii

We are what we come to by the River.
I having known mostly deserts cling
to any memory of water: its glint
a beacon no green valleys can dim.
Always my eye goes straight to the water,
no matter where I am. It is one of the marks
of a desert person to be obsessed by water.

iii

In the silence that comes internally,
the rustling of other animals is distant
assurance, the light, shadow mingling
as worlds try to meet, hover on peripheries,
geographies of momentary agreement,

all holding to what seems safe, possible.
A water snake raises his head, watches the shore.
Boy, he watches water snake while crow, he
fixes them both with his glassy black eye
and who's to say who watches them all?

Cow Dogs

The ranches I knew as a boy . . . .
It was the Depression then,
though as my father used to say,
"It's all we've ever known,
Depression, but we do all right."

Skinny steers and no market,
ranchers doing the hard work
because they've always done it,
waiting, nursing Durham butts,
cursing the lack of rain.

Even the dogs were thin
in those years. Dogs were part
of a ranch, guarding, yelping,
chasing chickens for sport
when nobody was looking, cocky

plume tailed dogs who looked like
four-legged cowpunchers, took
the same airs, the same lazy tensions
as they waited for action, any kind
of excitement. One old dog I remember

used to be able to throw a young calf
without hurting him much. In the evenings
the hands would gather and he would rise
slowly, carefully, walk to the corral
catch the calf running and throw him

neat as the devil into a cloud of early
evening dust. "It wasn't much," Old Jonesy
used to say, "but it sure as Hell
took your mind off your problems."

—Dust rising from the baked earth,
night settling on the silent ranch.

Virginio

—Old Town, 1930
Fort Sumner, New Mexico

Separate, lovely with lanterns
this adobe village stood a part
of Spain & laughter, wine.
Singing.

      Old men sat in the sun
talked to children of old days
of nothing at all. Virginio.
Rolling brown paper cigarros
told his stories while a new town
rose beside the Pecos River.

Even in 1930 his village
had its gamblers, cockfights,
bailes for quick feet, the dark
silks whirled, glittered in the night.
A laughter of girls, deep voices
of men, followed by a quietness.

We children of the new Anglo town
climbed the road, Virginio becoming
grandfather to us all, Spanish
& Anglo. We sat, ate tortillas
in the sun while our fathers worked
built a world with different
sounds: bulldozers, the clink of cash
in drawers. A measure. A worth.

Years passed, old walls
no longer slapped with river mud,
in springtime rains, fell. People
moved away, patterns changed
& Virginio, it is told, screamed
died, hiding in his daughter's
basement

    strange memories
    mocking him through
    a drunken dark, heavy
    with children's faces.

My Friend

The town called him sissy, laughed at him,
but behind his back. His eyes stilled laughter.
He embroidered, that's true. He was fat
and played few games, even when we were children.
I remember him always standing to the side,
watching with the quiet courage some disabled
people have when they see others perform actions
they themselves could never accomplish.

After the war, when I was in graduate school,
he called, set up a meeting in a bar. He was
surprised I drank, remembering my father
and how I'd sworn never to touch a drop but
things change he said softly, with understanding
as his boyfriend came out of the men's room
whining for money to play the jukebox and my friend
took some change out of his pocket and gave it
to the youngman and I saw once more how very far
we both were from anything resembling home.

He died somewhere in the Midwest. I have thought
of him for most of my life now. His death
in no way stops the thoughts. I see him now
just outside the action, calmly knowing
he could never play the right part, never
be more than the watcher, quietly smiling.

Village Ways

—are you now,
or have you ever been?"
from the old Loyalty Oath

In the hot sun of the Llano, the cool
shadows of arroyos, the question hangs
like that red-tailed hawk or the buzzard,
his mottled neck stretching out towards the sun.

I choose to let my nature, the contradictions
stay where they are . . . .

     In an earlier, simpler time
most people thought they knew who they were.
Folks identified each other by their grandfathers,
and by whether a person had travelled and how far.

"Old Joe's mother went to St. Louis once."
"She did!" And one knew that Old Joe's mother
was just a mite questionable. Good people stayed
put and usually died within a hundred yards
at most of where they were born and God help
them, whatever they did, they tried to hide
in the darkness of night time village streets
or the guttering of a coaloil lamp

     the hump of covers, the
loneliness of men, women who slept alone and called out
to Baptist gods or, worst of all, kept their silences,
died without ever hearing or speaking a word of softness,
or known the tremor or love, peace of sin but

"By damnation," as Jim used to say, "every stemwinding
sonofabitch knew who his grandpappy was and just where
he'd lie his own bones down which is a hell of a lot
more than most of them city folks can say!"

Maybe. But for me, the darkness still swirls
with question. The villages are pretty much gone and
who's to tell the dark-eyed ones now where their past
lies or the meaning of the fearful song the wind sings?

The People From The Valley

—for Frank Waters
in affectionate and grateful memory

The farmers come, come
on down the Pecos Valley
in busted-bottom wagons

their children thin
blonde cornhusk hair
blowing

Sparrows watch dry ruts
for spilled kernels
the men, stiff, formal

black suits, white shirts,
the women searching for
other wagons, bright bonnets

Cottonwood leaves clash
green in Saturday's wind
as the quiet children sit

aware they
will be watched by
town boys in their victor's clothes
the dark eyes of townsmen

watching for any beauty
the land has missed, its
women, this land hungers

for women, and for farmers
who can write their own obituaries
in the lines of their hard hands.

Blacky

He was a gambler, an old friend.
He lived in Old Town, up on the Hill.
One Sunday morning Dad & I

climbed into the Model A Ford, rattled
away. Near Lucero's we stopped, got down.
Blacky's there. "Hear you're

looking for me?" "Yes." Silence.
I walk a little bit away.
"You stole that pot."

"Prove it." Blacky reaches slowly
down & picks up a large rock.
He heaves it through the windshield.

The glass shatters, lines jagged
in the sun, spreading. My dad
looks at him, then hits him fast.

Blacky's body flies up and across
the hood, sliding into the glass, blood
raying, ran down in bright rivulets.

The next Saturday night they played
"Brother-in-Law" poker, won
forty dollars, backed out of the bar

together, no one dared stop them laughing
the two friends, high on bootleg whiskey,
their big fists cocked & ready.

Old Red

—for Stan and Nancy Noyes

It seems I am always writing
about dogs, or snakes, or crows.
Maybe it's because I find them
so much more interesting finally
than most humans with their ways
that lead so gracelessly to death.

Old Red. Big Irish setter (almost),
running like hell across the meadows
of my childhood, a ball or a stick
in his soft mouth, his eyes warm
me even now as I ruffle his ears
pick up the stick and throw it
clear to forever, where he lives.

My Greatuncle Bert

Almost every morning he left
dressed in old tweeds, cap, heavy
walking stick. He held his head

up, strolled down the dirt road,
stopped by the grocery store, selected
his box of long tubed Russian cigarettes

put them on the tab for his nephew
to pay for later, stalked off to the
Sundown Saloon where, very carefully,

he savored one shot glass of whiskey
after another, talking easily
of the money he had once had (true)

and of his adventures (mostly true)
his lean, grizzled face sagging slightly
as the country men politely moved away

leaving him to the terrible solitude
of the drunk, his lips still moving
over the words that shaped the stories

no one there or in the whole village
could either understand or listen to.
One night he fell, we found him

within the morning of a winter's sun
his blood on the rock doorstop, the high
blue of his eyes, fainter then,

his slender long fingers, heavily
nicotine stained but well-groomed
stretching out toward our closed door.

Grandmother

She with the pale blue gunfighter's
eyes, my father called them, sword
hungry, battle starred old Celts
would have said, she being one
of them, some lost high priestess
of Druidism spinning out Phenobarbital
dreams of past highland castles
and titles that turned to dust
before one even touched them.

She taught me to read when I
was three, sang me Bobby Burns
and skilled me in the Highland code, Scot
manhood, the grimmest of responsibilities
a Bushido in kilts and targes, Claymores and
Nec Flatu, Flactu Nec, "Neither wind
nor wave," can stop one of our family
or so said the blazon of the Edwards
MacEdward clan
                    Her eyes as she told
sword stories of Robert the Bruce, Wallace,
the Black Douglas and the wild skirl
of battlepipes calling the men to their laird
and often their deaths
                            leaving women
keening on the bare hillsides of the Highlands. She
died to haunt our house, walking the long hall
to my cold room, mourning outside, calling
all through Korea she stood by my side her face
lighted by our ship's red battlelamps, us at General
Quarters, she, my grim weird, my ancestral banshee

●◆

It was her voice I heard when
our old house creaked and groaned in the Llano
winds as my own battles drew near, and fierce
and bloody times came upon me.

Burro Man

I heard he went
away, old Maximiliano,
took his burros
down the trail one
day and never came
back

some say he died
others just shake their
heads and wonder what
he did down there

with sixteen burros
the world being
what it is today and no
room for burros
anywhere

Valleys, Valleys

Valleys!

        "Where there is
water." Pecos. The longing the
desert has for water grows toward
the centering pale muddy ribbon down
the middle of eroded springtime
valley

The burro moves slowly toward
the trough, sparkling water, algae green
on the galvanized lining. Steel windmill blades
slice the clean wind as we desert
creatures, who in large part are themselves
water, our own rivers running within
us, hear the noise in our own ears
begin at our fingertips and rush to our eyes
shining with water

        the isolate thirst of
valleys, surrounded by desert, its quick breathing

Day of the Snake

My sister, 3 years old in a pinafore sought
shade from our hard New Mexico sun, the white
blazes on the Hereford cattle at the line
camp, her under the one tree, beside the wind
mill

    —& a rock, beside her foot, out of
    shade, grew into awareness,
    a prickle at the back of . . .
    hesitation

    the moving coils
    dark tongue flicked
    out, back

an inch from her foot the rock flat head
steady eyes, her bare foot, vulnerability
of a baby before the sun

& how our father protested
when the rancher killed the heat passive snake
—a five foot Diamondback—he saying,
with perfect truth, he spared
my daughter, god damn it let
him live

Later, the snake's head crushed, spreading
to rock, rattles quivering musically
we walked
away, blazing suns
about our heads.

Moonlight on the Valley

The New Mexico hills move
dark blue shadows, leave senses
of history, of men and women walking
lonely trails, following the moon.

This moon reflects the face
of my father, the River speaks
in tongues of the long Dead.
In New Mexico all the land shifts

and subtly the footprints a person
makes, change. The talking wind
scars his flesh and how deeply cuts
the River and my father's voice.

Still Life

Three old New Mexican men
hunched back on their boot heels
smoke spitstuck brown Durhams
the white circle of paper, black
bull centered upon it, hangs from
each pocket like a badge, a coat
of arms

These old men watch the mountains
not each other, their stiff hats
hard above their eyes, they watch
the changing mountains, grow older.

—blue smoke curling up
to get lost in sky. Behind them
the rough wind & rain washed adobe
the straw yellow, jagged. In the clear
air the mountains rise up pale blue too.

The Dry Goods Store

with its window and the single mannequin,
dressed to a style a dozen years old in New York.
Racks of clothes, dusted each day, rarely sold.
He lived in back, darkly handsome, with his wife, one son.

The son grew tall and had gentle, sure eyes.
The mother thickened to ruin, while the father
shook hands, moved among the clothes, altered them
to fit at request, and one night died hurling

his car into a concrete pillar. His son on Bataan,
later in Korea, tied to a tennis court in winter,
came back, a sketch of his dead father, married
his nurse. A kind man, without rancor for his

sufferings. His mother and mine played Mah Jong,
bridge, talked without, to my memory, saying much,
waited as the evenings darkened above the pillar,
prayed for me to come home, blooded by another war

and the nights I spent wondering where the stone
column was that I would shatter myself against,
my tie as neatly knotted.

The Day of the Pig

—Sacramento Mountains 1940

One of them, grazing the still
meadow, slightly behind the others.
A man in our hunting party who wished,
despite warnings, "to have fresh pig
for supper"

      spotted domestics
gone wild, they were taller, heavier
than javelinas, meaner
my father said

      be ready to run
but there wasn't time, the fool
missed & the pregnant young sow, black spotted
white in the early dusk, charged
faster than I ever knew a pig could run,
low, the pounding of her sharp hooves

& I dropped to one knee, opened
fire: saw dust fly from .22 hits,
head on, pig coming, dust,
an angry snapping of teeth

until Dad's 30/30 slug caught her flush
& spun her down, blood trickling
from her relaxing snout

We cut her open, keeping an eye
to the rest of the sounder, dressed
her & later, beside a mesquite wood fire,
the man ate shining piglets
one after the other, saying
how delicious they were, smacked
his lips and laughed, sun already
down—a clear moon lighting
a still mesa.

Anastasio Murillo

A man of parts—of birth, lineage.
I used to wait for him, hiding
behind mesquite bushes, leap out
begging him to let me go to school early.

He was a kind man, my father's friend,
so he said one day, "Si, Hijito, tu puedes,"
a simple gesture for him, opening to
an eternity for me. All those years

full of rooms, sweaty disinterested bodies.
The weariness of his eyes should have
told me, I should have caught some awareness
of the centuries that lie behind momentary

knowing: I was starting a long journey,
he finishing one. Superintendent of Schools,
don Anastacio, heir to an appointed job,
hidalgo de los llaneros, he held my hand

and walked me back to my father's house,
told him of the promise he had made, hugged
me and left me alone to confront those faces
that turned as I entered, the frozen smile

of the teacher, I, too young, forever too young
for the pressure of all those books. He knew that.
I still turn the pages of books, his face
occasionally before me. Outside the rivers

dry up, the sky clouds, but not with rain.
Thin birds circle the dying cow and what message
is there in the pages for me as the years catch me up
and the thunder of blood dims my ears?

The Day of the Crow

1

The small sharpness of a boy's life.
My father whistling crisp and clear
as out of the Southwest's sunshine
Karl came winging, cawing about his needs.

Raw beef, bloody still from the knife,
chunks of bologna, cheese, civilized
bird of carrion, he perched lightly
upon my hand, flexing his hard talons

—the time he streaked silently down
to attack my mother's new Easter hat
rip the feather off, tear the felt, screeching
out his rage and triumph over her tears.

"How would you feel," my little sister asked,
"if a crow wore a human skin before you?"
And Mother listened for that was the way
she was and it was Easter just the same.

2

Karl, his eye cocked, watched us eat
what he would never touch, we laughing
at his cleverness, his tricks and thefts.
Pens, knives flew glittering with his cries

as my own world grew crowded with the long days
of summer and coyotes, eagles my father found
and we returned later, grown, healthy to the land
they owned and we only shared, the sleek brush

of Karl's black wings against my face stayed,
though he flew, he flew in black crowds of crows,
mated I think and slashed the clear light
back to my waiting hand. Then once

the crows flew by, unswerving, headed away
and out. My father found them later, circling
on the ground in their funeral dance, cawing
softly for the shotgunned figure that we buried
observing our rites, not theirs, on a cool evening
when sharp stars cut holes in a summer's night.

Night

How still the Llano is in full moon.
Light is everything here, a new world
come into focus, no movement at all.

The silver grass, pale hills at the edge
of the cap rocks. Down there, the Rio.
There, the Military Road where the Kid
still walks, moon glints for eyes, stalking
whatever memory he had that he holds dear.

The old men sit by the store and talk
and talk, maybe spitting to show they
still remember, have feelings, and are
not as dead as they are beginning to look.

Later they sleep, the Llano moon locked
outside, the curtains of their windows
hang magically, keep all loneliness out.

River Bottom

where as boys we played in beds of quicksand,
teasing with it as it sucked our feet down, one boy
always standing clear to help as it slowly crept up
our ankles, to our knees, nearly to our hips.

Then the shouts of laughter as we'd fall forward,
float on the greyish water that rose through the sand,
wiggle our ways out. Jimmy (killed in WWII),
Tom (became a drunk), Juan (died in a barrio in
Albuquerque from knife wounds), me, still feeling
the suction of those sands

A Lament for Old Cowboys

—The Goodnight-Loving Trail
Which passes near Fort Sumner

They hear voices, the old
whispers, the blued
hoof beats of their horses shatter
the stone arroyo's silence

       beside the mountain
       in soft mesquite dusk
       the flutter of eagle feathers
       shadows of old ceremonials

Under concrete and asphalt
under these years of dust and longing
there are tracks: bobcats with high
yellow eyes, mountain lions, wolves
the smaller creatures fleeing before
them . . . .

Peel the road back and see
where the young cowpunchers passed
whooping, going to see the Elephant
riding the Tiger, hearing the Owl
hoot along trails we never found
the ending of

       the old voices of this land
sing in guitared darkness, cry and moan
as the wind rises, dust down an empty
road bright with moonlight, scudding clouds

The Day of the Sculptress

She got off the train at dusk,
her silken dress blowing gently,
I knew she must be pretty then,
though I was too far away to see.

She came from the EAST, was my
mother's family, had some of the MONEY.
Still, she was far away, talked strangely,
hardly noticed me. I was about six then,
in second grade and I watched her slenderness

as I watched watersnakes in the irrigation
ditch, lovely, but not to be touched.
One day they called the school together
and we all listened to her, my cousin,

as she showed her sculptures, talked,
somehow I understood, perceived, grew
proud as her real life flashed, dimmed.
Later that day I came around the house

she was bathing naked in a great tub,
she saw me, laughed, waved me closer,
I remember the soap on her skin, her small
smooth breasts and nipples, marbled

by memory, I can't picture her eyes,
only her hands as they stroked me.
How angry my mother was, how strangely
guilty Father looked, putting her on the train
as it pulled out into the blazing days
that lay before us all . . . .

The Town Planner

—for Keith Wyman Edwards

Almost every village had one,
a dreamer, full of visions.
Ours was my uncle, his pictures
cluster about his memory. One,
taken graduating from law school.
Another, him at a picnic shows
an army camp double-exposed above.
Date: 1916. Place: Pecos River.

To him, Fort Sumner would become a city
larger than Albuquerque, El Paso,
the other cities that grew in the mind
from rail heads, mesas of waving grasses.
I still remember street signs
stretching out to desolation across
unsold, empty land neatly cut into lots
no one ever bought, as the rails went on
gleaming, towards the next sunset, the
next man who seized his vision, saw
his own city of the future . . . .

My uncle. Handsome, intense with clear
blue skies behind him, I remember the dam
he got built, him shaping a golf course
out of a mesquite flat, with oiled sand
greens, his sure sense of history
and of what was to come from his own
undoubted greatness. I am left

with his greatness. The town is still
here, small, its lights graceful in the dusk,
green in the summer splendor of the River.
Somewhere I am sure he still pushes on
a drink in his fist, dreams in his dead eyes.

Tomasino

Who was a good man in some village
where I lived, sometime, who knew
the secret names of the hills, the valleys.

When he spoke of earth, it lighted
like the yes that he carried always
in his eyes, his hands outstretched

in welcome. A poor man. Tomasino,
who lived a frugal life on his farm
but his arms were strong, his face

even today, long after, is the flare
of a match struck to light a lantern,
or the race of brown water down

a furrow when the irrigation gate
is first opened among the spring flowers.
So do I remember him, standing in a field

saying "It will rain soon, the tomatoes
will grow and the winter will be late
this year, the birds will sing songs

and not eat tomatoes." Most of it
didn't happen but such was the faith
of Tomasino that I can see his eyes now.

The Rattlesnake

whose old eyes watch
whose flat head shines
like brittle glass quick

flicks! his dark tongue
it senses his world and me
desert man

see, I reach out my hand
almost to you with no malice
the hot air stands waves between us.

The Powerhouse

My dad worked there, part-time, knew about
as much as any of the other guys, excepting always
Smokey Lewis who ran it, nursed and cursed it,
keeping the big generators whining and rumbling
from about six o'clock in the afternoon
until about nine in the darkening evening.

I used to sit on the floor of our kitchen
and watch the bare bulb where it hung from
the porcelain insulator on two cloth covered wires,
saw it begin to glow just after I heard the voice
of the powerhouse start to sound from across
the village, near the River. When the bulb
was firmly incandescent, I relaxed my vigil
went to help Mother set the table for evening
thinking of daddy down there

              where, according to him
great balls of static electricity sometimes rolled
across the floor like Taos witches but could pass
right through a man's leg without harming him. Or
one stormy night, how there was a short in the cables
that led through a cement tunnel to the main transformer
and how he had crawled into the tunnel, just to see
what the hell was happening, maybe find where the short
was and got fired out of that tunnel like a big bag
of cloth and bones and if it hadn't been for Smokey
who knew some artificial respiration, he'd have been
deader than any door nail . . . .

To me, the voice of the powerhouse sounded like a great wolf, baying over the houses and the people. I was fascinated by it, but always its presence touches me with vague fear—fewer and fewer coal oil lamps glowed in the evenings, the noise grows and electric bulbs watch out of more and more windows, their eyes steady and purposeful through the dark of a winter night beside the Llano.

Lem Lyons

When I get as old as he was,
I sure hope I hang on to the same graces.
Prospector, hermit, he always made me
welcome when I hiked across the mesa.

Fixed me coffee, keeping one blue eye
on the falling sun and just on time
he'd say I'd better be heading home
and I always made it—as the shadows
led ahead of me I would see the light
in my mother's window, the pale aura
of her coaloil lamp on dusty glass.

I don't know when he died. I was gone.

The Grain of Sand

—for Jim Harris & Hawk

There he goes, old hawk, he touches
the thermal, rises, lifts himself to dot
sky bending in a semicircle of blue heat.

The grey shimmer of mirage standing unbroken
until the strike

        down he drops knocking
a buck rabbit off his feet, flurry of dust,

rises again, talons blooded,
crippled rabbit hiding in the sage and brush
for coyotes to find:

        desert, crawling under heat,
slick glass sand tumbles in little avalanches and
the tarantula flashes back, her catch firmly
in her hairy mandibles. The quick awkward gait
of the Giant Desert Scorpion. His more deadly
kin, the straw colored Durango, all cocked, waiting

as this desert sun goes down, as blue, grey
and pink spread themselves to silence and I hear
tiny feet and scales flee the hunting night.

In New Mexico Territory,
As Best I Understand,

The lights were softer, dangers
came more unannounced, more dashingly dressed.

There was a silence, surrounded by a violence,
potential, lethal, always from the shadows.

The distances between towns, the hard roads,
let the men, though they damned each other,

hardly ever meet, but then came the swift swift shots
of eyes, the clenched fists . . . .

It all began with men, and with women
edging, nudging them on. Perhaps the horses

were partly to blame, the killings sent the horses
wild, they danced on their white-stockinged feet

in their great eyes gunfire flashed and rolled.
Now we have all this. The gunfighters still hold

the cities and some of the towns. The horses are
mostly gone and it is the land that is dying.

My coyote friends and I sit separate in darkness
watching the winking lights. We remember.

Valley of The Río Chama

—near Ghost Ranch, Rio Grande Institute

The River, small at Fall, drifts through cottonwoods,
greypinkblue hills, dropping slowly
down past Abiquiu, Española on its way to the sea

leaves, twigs, pieces of the mountain life upstream
carried along like picture postcards, or paintings

All this great flow, color, wind, light is center
that has to be for something deeply anciently holy:

           the leaves are
masks, the twigs dancing legs and arms, held
spun to the beat of River and an earth swirling under
the weakening autumnal sun of harvest promise
before the high mountain winter comes with its own
icy mask
    Most of us here today are artists of some
sort, all caught embarrassed before this magnificence,
these glories of canyons, bluffs carved into standing
hooded figures, multicolored giant crayons the sun
has melted until they stand layer upon layer
in rich pastel, as if a prism had broken strewing
raw light into colors, freezing them there in sand
stone clay

    We walk away, murmur to each other of the
weather, our small arts, our tiny worlds of
imitation, longing that only we can inhabit.

●◆

My new friend, a painter, says, "I'm old enough to know
better than to try painting all that!" and shakes his head.
But colors are words the voices of rock and canyon speak.
How can they not be spoken? How can we not listen?

—seeing the stream, hearing the leaves golden and
brown in their own falling splendor, earth holding
all in Her cupped hands of rock and color and
light.

The Arroyo

He walked there with his buddy
both carried .22's, hunting rabbits
for supper—down Yeso Creek, thin
slick stream running down
the center of the eroded arroyo.

He was close to the bank's edge
when out of the brush a heavy stick
fell towards him, no rattle, just
struck. He leaped, dropping his
rifle and yelled as the bank crumbled
under him, the giant diamond
back just missing him.

He picked himself up
looked around. Snakes uncoiling everywhere
from their winter hibernation slid across
the sand and all around him the whirring
rattles began. Angry, hungry the snakes
probed, hard flat heads back, cocked, rattles
thundering in the draw as the sand slid grated
under his boots. Then he stood perfectly still.

Crack! The head of the nearest snake dissolved
into pulp, its body thrashed wildly, nearly touched him.
"Don't move. Everything will be ... Crack! all right.
Now just you ... Crack! ... Stand there, bueno?"

The barrel of the single-shot .22
was too hot to touch when his friend
finished. Later the two counted 11 snake
bodies, 5 or 6 that got away.

—For my father

The Token

ligera, ligera
        tu cuerpo es la huella
            de tu cuerpo . . . .
              —Octavio Paz

In a dream my long dead uncle came to me,
he of my name, a heritage as twisted
as the swollen Pecos in flood time.

I was giving a poetry reading somewhere,
we drove into the town, I saw the bare hill
behind the town. Later, a message came:

"Your uncle awaits you at the Grand Hotel."
I was driven to the huge building that now
covered the same hill. The desk clerk said,

"Hurry, he's waiting in 301." My aunt, living
then, opened the door and impatiently let me in,
indicating a closed door behind her.

I open it and there is my uncle's whole law office,
walls filled with walnut desk, leather bound books,
him sitting, his grey Stetson on, behind the desk.

Taller than I remembered, his face
greyly elegant, with sharp aristocrat
bones, pale blue eyes looking far off.

Gray frost crystals powdered his cheeks.
A force like the pressure of water
compelled my lips, I knew the crystals

were death, yet I kissed them, my uncle
never looking at me, his eyes distant
certainties where strange birds flew, crying.

Don Juan Seguro Que Sí

An old man, of some dignity, he became known
by the way he answered nearly every question
in English or Spanish—seguro que si!,
with a big smile but of course he didn't always
do what he had promised to do, and that was
understood, accepted.

        Sir John "Sure, that's OK"
might be an English equivalent, but not quite.
The Spanish ripples off the tongue, holds affection,
warmth and easy promise, now nearly forgotten
in the land of mañana which held my childhood:

Don Juan, friend of my family, broke rancher,
driven to town by drought, too much high living,
a wife he loved that died. He used to wave
at everybody who passed by, him sitting
on his small porch. That was how they knew
when he died. He just didn't come out
one morning, he was gone, but they found
he'd paid the undertaker, selected his coffin,
and hired the priest, seguro que si!

Tableau

I have a picture in my mind, father holding Daisy,
his cocker spaniel, both sinking deep into quicksand.
We were walking together when he, in his way,
went his way, leaving me to find them later.

He'd heard Daisy yelping, found her in the sands,
leaped in to save her. For a moment I couldn't believe
he'd done it, my desert and river wise father, but
there they were, a man and his dog, slowly going down
as the sun also sank.

       It took me an hour to get them out,
reaching with my hand from a rock on the bank, helping
him, still holding the dog, to edge closer to safety.
By the time he was free and clear, Daisy barking at
the grey sands, it was almost dark as we picked our way
out of the bosque, beating with yucca sticks against the
ground to let the rattlers know we were coming. Whack!
And a rattle would come from close by, then slightly
away, Whack!, and more would buzz, the cool evening air
       bringing them out to hunt.

       He sent Daisy ahead of us finally,
"She could smell 'em better," he said, though the
cucumber musk of snake seemed everywhere to my nostrils
as we climbed up the hill and headed for the old car
parked against the growing darkness.

       Dad stalked out like John Wayne
after a victorious gunfight. Daisy and I, trailing
along behind still watching for the striped shadows
of snakes, moon rising on a hunting world.

The Day of the Calf

The dark grasses of the mesa stand hot & stiff
with late summer. The draws fill with cattle
lowing, questioning, pushed along by cowhands
who know too well the work that awaits this drive.

              Ahead, the branding
fires, we squat around them, smoking.
One or two boys, uneasy, wipe their hands
on their Levis, watch the nearing cattle.

The first calf is cut out, runs ahead, is cut
back again by the cowsmart pony, is roped,
deftly thrown: his bellows, heard close
are deafening. His tongue lolls, thick slobbers
about his lips. He's pig-tailed now. A man
walks quickly forward, holds horn cutters. Snip.
Snip. The two budding horns fly off, jets of blood.

The other man takes his pocket knife, reaches down
slashes the sac, pulls the slippery balls out
cuts them free, the calf's eyes rolling with
shock, twisting in its agony as tar is daubed
heavily into the bloody cavity by the boy.

             The calf, freed, rises
unsteadily, wanders around, yelling deep
in his chest for his mother and the boy wipes
his tar stiff hands on his levis, moves toward
the next calf which is already down.

Cow Country Ceremony

A lonely clapboard church on the mesa
comes suddenly to life as pickups roll in,
lights switch on and smoke starts to rise
from the chimney

                           a fiddle scratches a note
just to test the air, a guitar tunes up, the old
piano plays a honky-tonk tune. Elderly ranchers
and their plump wives wait till the music changes
slows to old-time pieces and they lumber out two
stepping into space where the pews used to be and
my son, just about 8, who has gone to Mescalero Apache
Mountain Spirit Dances, Santo Domingo Corn Dances,
Taos Eagle Dances and Yaqui Deer Dances all his short life
whispers worriedly into my ear, " Dad, they don't really think
that is a dance, do they?"

The Old Man At Evening

i

Which world should I speak of?
The one by the Pecos River, volumes of sound,
the wind through cedars, echoes of rabbits,
their dying cries, or the quick memories
of wolves?

I know with whatever sadness
the truth of lamplight in autumn,
the sandpaper brush of lips,
women that believe in some strength
held, secretly, against the darkness.

I know I have lived before.
It is etched in me, modes of responses,
awarenesses that some others have and I
love you, knowing we have touched before,
coupled, talked, our eyes not unremembered
as the centuries concealed our true faces
and we made love with our imaginings.

ii

I am he who calls
the night, yet I
forget the words

in the darkness
we are all afraid
lose touch, lost

I know whatever
I say gets swallowed
by something in the night

my love
the complicated stars
sometimes seem

to spell out your name
I do not know how
to answer them, hold

you close, my lips
trembling as I try
to speak the correct

charm, the final phrase
before their light
I speak this love for you

Llano Estacado

Yucca stalk. Hard spikes
below in green slashes they
mark a drying land.

1864

Down there Kit Carson
leaves the Navajos & the
Apaches, end of the Long
Walk.

The warriors try to be
farmers, dig ditches,
many die. Yucca stalks

their roots, deep
down in the cool moisture
they twist among the bones
of sunken mountains

1908

Over there my grandfather
arrives from Omaha
with his wagon, his kids
& almost no supplies, money

while this earth flashes
away in showers of mica
whistling dust

—Old Fort Sumner
New Mexico Territory

The Day Of The Dog

He'd been appointed Town Marshal.
We boys, expecting Wyatt Earp, got him.
Almost fifty, fat with a red sweating face
& drunkard's eyes, he wore a dirty shirt
old trousers and shoes with no socks.

My uncle said his wife was a nice woman,
and they gave him the job to keep him out of trouble.
There wasn't much in the Village, a few punchers
fighting on Saturday night, once in awhile a drunk
to jail. Morgan handled drunks real well. "He knows
the way," one man said, laughing.

One day the Town Council told him to run
the stray dogs out of town because of rabies.
Since the old man could hardly walk, much
less run, they asked us to catch the dogs,
bring them to a pen and then, they said,
he'd take a pickup load off and come back
for the rest. A friend of mine asked, "How
come there's no cage to put on the pickup?
Them dogs will jump right out, you know
they will." But we didn't listen.

By four in the afternoon, we had 20 or 30 dogs,
males and bitches in the pen. Old Morgan drove
up, got out. We could see he was drunk, his
hand shook when he took out the slim .38 and
started firing blindly into the massed dogs.
Some of the kids yelled for him to stop
but he just reloaded and kept shooting, bullets
screaming off through the streets, men diving
for cover and the dogs howled, their blood running
in little rivers over the hard clay, him weaving
as he aimed the pistol, his star glinting in
the sun, the noise of each shot like a crashing
blow. Solemn, drunk, he did his duty and no one
dared stop him until the dogs were all lying there
dead or dying. Then the mayor strode up, took the gun
and led him back to his wife who cried all the time
he told her how he'd fixed those dogs,
hadn't he, honey?

The Valley At Night

The sweet ache of sleeping children.
Wind outside, the window gently rattling,
and how the mind fills with stories, told,
untold, without a hint of what that head
small, vulnerable, against the pillow dreams.

Someday, perhaps on a far planet, I know my heart
will return to these moments and I will puzzle
my head with longing: now, I touch the soft hair
kiss the forehead, reluctantly turn out the light.

The Rock Collector

Old Doc Allison, a "doctor" in fun
or grudging respect

              a hard drinker
with kindness and more knowledge
than we could cope with—Saver
of Small Boys, tortured cats,
dogs with tin cans on their tails

—walking uncertainly down Main
Street, faultlessly dressed, his hat
brushed and slightly tilted, the cold
glare of the drugstore light caught
his red face, the deep lines . . . .

He was once a famous geologist
the town said. We boys didn't care
sensing in him the living boy, the
comrade by the way he talked to the night
(his many kindnesses, the shy looks)

When he died his wife threw out his
specimens, quartz, jagged crystal
more beautiful than diamonds, copper
ores, rare gem stones embedded in matrix
caught sparkling in the sun of the alley-
way's dust

We boys gathered them up
set them in an oval about his grave
on the Hill, watched the late sun
pick out the lights while the lamps
of the town darkened beneath us
and age caught us each up, glowing
in the new starlight, the hanging
dust . . . .

Curriculum Vitae

desde la sangre
de las estrellas,
nacido

In some such way was I born, outsider
to three cultures, parted by the blood
of all, the wind's chants are blessings
somehow I know that, touch bird wings

with my eyes the canyons grow heavy
too light, too light, the air blazes
with memories that bear the future:
mountain roses, Indian paintbrushes, daisies

all caught up in this fingerprint of mine
at the least me, at the most, what I
might become, given enough seasons
enough winters to crack my face properly

Portrait of a Father

My father was a hard man, closed
off from what he could not understand.
One night he tried to pry off the ring
from my mother's hand, she in a coma,

he with a new woman waiting for the bright
glimpse of diamond in the darkened room—
it flashed and mother sighed, moved
as he slipped back through the door.

He walked tall, had big hands, quick
smile—"Could charm the ears off a mule,"
his brother said, knowing him too well.
I remember the smell of smoke and cedar.

Men would follow him anywhere, it was said
they covered for him when he disappeared
into alcoholic odysseys along the Mexican Border,
whores and drunken fights two weeks long.

I remember him smelling of vomit and urine,
barely alive for days, then him striding out
his big shoulders straight, blue eyes
with diamond glints in the hard sun.

Surrounded by dust, roar of Caterpillar
engines, waving his hands, conducting work
into a symphony of labor and the rough road
emerged from violated land, was polished to

smooth asphalt right down to the thin white
stripe that ran on to forever. My father,
moving on, saying little, his green felt hat
scrunched down over his eyes, bent slightly

as if he walked against a stiff wind, the world
always at his back, neck muscles tensed, expectant,
a fighting man Snort Woods said "who couldn't tell
an enemy from a friend, what was his from what was /not

I remember the dust of the desert, the smell
of engine oil. The way his hands held a coyote pup
and how he laughed as the pup struck out, the white
flashing teeth flickering like gems in the dry air.

The Dog Poisoner

To this day, no one knew who he or she really was.
All we kids knew was that it came in the night,
little balls of hamburger (then you could buy it
three pounds for a quarter and my mother made me tell
the butcher is was for my dog but we ate it)
came over the fence, lay there and real soon
a dog was there writhing in pain. Ground glass

was all it ever used and we hated it, would I'm sure
have killed it if we could ever have caught it.
Forgive me for saying "it," but who could think
of such a creature as an animal or even a human?
My mother said once what it really wanted was to kill
a human, a boy or a girl, but hadn't enough courage.

We boys finally banded together and patrolled the huge
vacant lots that separated our homes but all we ever
got was tired and our parents made us stop, even though
the killings went on.

                    One day they just quit. It happened
that the day before an old man who lived down towards
the Valley got sick and died, vomiting blood.
The Doc said he didn't know what killed him but we did.
It got its hamburger mixed up and God forgive me we
were so glad we got out and danced in a circle,
shouting as if it were raining or some other miracle
had happened and nobody went to its funeral, nobody.

Spring

—for my compadre Rudy Anaya
Who grew up on the Pecos too

All night he could hear the noise.
In the morning, the plains lay
like pages of sunlight, no wind.
He hurried past the village,
through the Breaks, saw the crest
come down, heaving, adobe earth,
carrying uprooted trees, parts
of wooden houses from upstream.

The Rio Pecos had gone crazy again.
Rio Loco, the old man had called it once.
Quicksand in the Summer, floods in the Spring,
dry as hell in Winter. Rio Loco.
Ought to build a dam, the old man said.
Stop that crazy river in its tracks.
Now he could see what Old Tom meant.
A heavy snake gutting the Valley.

A young girl in a pinafore, pale
silk hair spun by him, her arms out
stretched, blue eyes open, was gone
before his muscles could even tense,
whirled away, turning and turning
into the dark water and he knew
through his trembling that this
was the first Spring he had ever known
with some kind of truth and backed up
quickly as the River ate the land
from under his feet, passed him by.

The Old Man & His Snake

The two lived there, almost together—
he in the shack, the snake below under
the warped floorboards in the cool darkness
cut by rays of light from the lamp above.

A thick Diamondback, nearly six feet long,
it moved out in moonlight to stalk rabbits
and rats. Out his window the old man pointed;
"There he goes, not enough to feed him around
here no more. Ain't had a rat or a mouse
in near two years. He's the reason, Old
Snake!"

    The two of them, growing older, keeping
careful distances from each other, geographies
of agreement (the old man stayed in at night,
the snake never went out in the day . . . .)

The old man pointed to his chamber pot. "Bought
that to keep from tangling with him. Can't use
the outhouse at night. Kill him? Why the hell
do that? He's got a right to live, ain't he?
Besides, I always know he's there, down under
the boards, hear him move every once in awhile,
and there's worse critters than snakes
lots worse than snakes . . . ."

—for Lem Lyons

Bridge Over The Pecos

There was this story about a railroad bridge.
Eleven men died, fell into the wet concrete pillars
were left there, stone men holding up the ties
spikes, the shining rails.

                Others say white men
killed them. They were black, story goes, one
for each pillar, for luck, for the blood
that binds stone and locks it into place.

Later, a switching engine fell when the roadbed
shifted, it tumbled steaming, its bright wheels
whirling suns, fell its heavy black arc
into quicksand

                Crew, engine and all sank beneath
the grey/silver sands and are down there yet, dead
hand near the throttle.

                Sun, rising over the Pecos, wind
wild in the cedar breaks, rabbits catching the scent
of foxes on their twitching noses, river run muddy
clouding the old stories, blurring the faces . . . .
How many deaths it takes to move a people across
a land

                Bridge, dead black marching pillars
The bronze sun, Indian songs beside, the quiet river.

—For my father
who knew the river
better than I

Brother & Sister Dancing: Cantina

—and the Mariachis are playing

Here we are
dancing out the wild songs, the heritage
our feet touch when our souls
dare not trespass.

The sharp note climbs, and high.

His trumpet catches in
smoky light, is an explosion against
his straining face, his great hat, the
racing gilded laces are real silver in the light

& all the while the dancers
whirl, mariachis sing
of revolution, love

Here is a center formed
by you and me, the others break
around us, strangers, agonies
of music snapping between
passing . . . .

—For Marjorie Ann

The Voice Of The Earth Is My Voice

—from a Navajo prayer

And we are the syllables on Her tongue,
Bright words held to the clear water, the soft
Marbled coloring of sandstone, framed in wind.

We are of the Earth and should never bravely
Forget or fail to give thanks to the dust
That bore us here, speaking, the voice of whirlwind

Knows our names, holds us past the time we imagine.
In no way less than the Earth, nor greater
Our eyes hold canyons, and willows, we last and last.

A Poem For My Newly Dead Father

We are risen out of the dusty
trails of our ancestors, as you were,
all men shaping footprints
that take years to conceive.

I had written you a book and then,
another, formed with words you
helped teach me. You put those stories
to my lips and passed on, not caring

or caring too much, I cannot say
what I will tell the small world
of you that lies within these white
white pages untouched by your hand.

July 4, 1972

Desert Cenote*

There is sadness among the stones
today, the rabbits are silent.

No wind. The heat bears down.
It has not rained for one year.

We have faith out here, desert
people, we wait, knowing with sureness

the swift cross of clouds, the blessings
of moisture (to deprive a man is to give

charms to him). I love this dry land
am caught even by blowing sand, reaches

of hot winds. I am not the desert
but its name is not so far from mine.

* Spanish-Aztec for "water hole, oasis"

Bone Knowledge

There's a quality about New Mexico
a certain sadness, light gathering
about a mountain, the buzz of gnats
over a spot of wet sand in an arroyo.

For years there was nothing here to exploit,
we lived with the grace of poverty about us
in a kind of shining penitence, a forgive
me attitude for we had not taken more

nor given less, we were whole, complete
in the silence of our evenings, the sun
lit extravagance of early mornings, bird
calls that echoed the sun's rising.

The sadness I suppose comes from change,
Heraclitus' river, not the same river,
not the same foot, as we became valuable
because of the very space that had protected us.

That hawk, circling the cap rock, though.
How will I explain to him, the changing air?

The Way Things Are Going

New Mexico will soon have passed away,
gasping like a minnow on a clay bottom of the Pecos.
I know, I feel the same. The air drifting up
from El Paso, down from Albuquerque, East from Tucson
West from Odessa is heavy, hangs like plastic rock
above us I know

      nothing but that beauty is the most
transitory while ugliness lasts and lasts. One comes
to hail the shining moment for what it is: one scale
of one tiny minnow flashing in the dying light, one face
—so loved—aging in this still brilliant, holy Sun.

Horsehead Crossing
South of Fort Sumner

Rented Room

You are the sound.
Your voice. I kept
wondering . . . .

          You were here
all the time. Behind
the sofa, back of the
mirror.

My father died
4th of July
hit to the heart
quickly, mercifully
by a clot of blood
too small to see.

He had lived a hard hour
or two, took generally
what he wanted, needed,
thought rarely of anyone.
The smile on his Irish face
twisted to grimace.

My mother stayed   with
us, no matter what he did
She died slowly of cancer.

I don't know who
 you are in this room
but I thought of them
the pain falling silently
night upon dusty windows

New Mexico

I claim all these years
as my own
        the land
its faces, shifting
in autumnal winds—
always there are far horizons

—old stories, cigars
the gleam of brandy
in a crystal glass

I claim all sadness
all joy

I claim
a tattered photograph
of my grandfather
in Territorial days

skidding across the yard
in springtime winds

I claim
my children, marching
solemnly to radio music,
growing older, I touch
my face, (so much like
his)

the years claim me
as I accept them, claw
marks lining my skin
while a Cooper's hawk
hits out for the high blue,
mountains gleam like prophecies
behind him, slashing the light.

I claim him too
for he bears my heart.

For All Daughters

The soft beauty of a child
gathers about you
as you take her
into your arms.

Knowing the fragility of her blood
the remorseless march of your seconds
you hold her tight, rocking to
your own inward winds of fear.

You two are one tower, one great
leaning together of stones resisting
time as best the two of you can.
A man is immortal, fearless when

he holds his daughter, is silhouetted
against the edge of the horizon, black
shapes on grey, when he holds her tightly
in his arms he is very strong

The Arrival of My Mother

—New Mexico Territory, 1906

She got off, according to her diary,
dressed in a lovely beaded gown, fresh
from Washington with sixteen trunks of ball gowns
chemises, blouses (4 Middie), shoes and assorted
lingerie. She was at that time about 25, old
for an unmarried woman. Her stiff mother was at
her side, she also wildly overdressed for New Mexico
sun and wind.

What must she have thought, seeing my uncle standing
hat in hand in the dust of that lonely train station
cracked yellow paint, faded letters of welcome
for passengers who rarely come?

The buckboard was waiting and they rode out into
the darkness of evening toward the tent and the half
built frame homestead house, wind dying as the sun
sank birdcries stilled.

I see her now out-shooting my father and me, laughing
at our pride and embarrassment. My sister, as good a
shot, waiting her turn. Or that picture of her
on horseback, in Eastern riding clothes beside the Pecos.
A picnic when I was small and how my father lifted me up
to her and she carefully walked the horse around rock
and sand.

          I suppose she finally arrived in New Mexico
in the April of one year when my sister and I sat beside
a rented bed, each holding one of her hands and watched
her eyes go childlike, unmasked as a kachina
entering the final kiva of this Dance. The graceful
the slim laughing woman of my childhood. The old mother
heavy with years slipped away and the woods of New
England dimmed as these dry hills ripened and caught
her last breath, drums, drums should have sounded
for the arrival of my mother.

The Encircled Grove

And written here is the ceremony of the land
itself, without commentary, other than what it,
this grove, places before the senses. In the deep cool
of glades, clumps of twisted salt cedar, snake
barked cottonwoods with trunks twice as thick
as a man, broad leaves pushing at the sunlight
that only glimmers down to the moist earth
with its beetles and ferns.

The grove is circular out of ancient incantation,
some enchantment older than Comanche spoke here,
formed this protected world and held it against
wind or geology. The high plain stops at the edge
of its greenness, swirls around it, continues
as far as the eye travels the spreading land
and domed blue hold it in their rushing powers.
Sky Father. Earth Mother. Here is the point
equidistant, focused, the navel that magic flows
through

            As I passed through
shaped, protected, set free by the Pecos River
and the wind from the quarrels of family, whispers
that held our old house fast. Grandmother's ghost
could never walk in the Bosque where silence became
a moistness, held your breath like another pair
of murmuring lips

—*for my brother, Simon Ortiz*

Songs For Dawn & Evening

—in thanks to Grandfather

i

I am glad
the sun has risen!
I get up
stretch
and with my
breathing
hail
what stands
behind the sun.

ii

I am glad
the sun has gone!
Now I hear
the universe
breathe back,
embrace darkness
and know that silence
the Ancient Ones spoke of
—though they must have
laughed when they said it
all those coyotes
and that irrigation pump

the way the stars cry out
just about midnight

— & for Mateo Amado Littlebird
— & my brother Harold

Abiquiu Poems

Rio Grande Institute
Ghost Ranch, 1985

i

Here among the creams, the tans of pastel sandstone,
where spirit faces speak out of light and shadow
on the strata—God's fingerprints on sheer cliffs

Rock speaks
up through the hand, the eyes:
its cold currents flow into my blood
touch bone

what a man takes to himself
as I said somewhere before, becomes him,
with age, the droppings of time
are all we can ever truly hold
outside but in, in, inside the words are
all flame, I can feel the layering
of those rocks as if they were the tissues
my own skin . . . .

The rocks are mine, as I grow theirs.

Both of us sensing our correspondences,
our fragile geographies

ii

I seem never alone up here. All of my people
walk fatally within me. Scotch/Irish/Welsh vagabond fighters
serious hard-eyed farmers, my mother's languid people
with their estates, their boredom, their drinking.
They're all hiding here, inside, pop out when least
needed.

●◇

I watch small War Chief play. He is two, walks
with the heavy grace of a Corn Dancer. Picks up stick,
hefts it. Good, he nods. Tries it out on larger boy.
I tell his father, my friend, "You guys could have used
a warrior like that a hundred years ago." He nods
and rushes to rescue his son's friend.

Or the man with penitente eyes. How he plays the pito
the thin, high fluted call that splatters like blood
over the room where he is standing wooden and alone.

We are, God forgive us, all New Mexican. We try to live
among, in spite of, the hatred of the past & all this
beauty, that which separates us, binds us together:

the chains of our bondage, keys to our freedom
—it is this land. This land. The last of the sunrays
strike the butte now. For a second, my mother's face
reflects there, then children

iii

—the children!

the lights within their eyes
Christmas trees, piñatas, ritual fires
reflect red, green, yellow, clear
up there through and past the trees

& the songs the land makes

(whether we are there or not:
let he/she who has ears
          sing back
          cauterize the darkness
          deepening into brain
          cleansing the blood's reign

and turn away, back to the faces
the hands, the walking bodies
moving through strata of hours
no different one from the other.
What is there to hate, each
being, part of the same?

We try to sing, for that is what we are given
commanded to do. Offer up our voices, eventually,
ourselves. We remain just as old as these rocks,
hold eternity like a rattle in our hands,
the darkening sky no darker than our eyes.

                    iv

I am alone, I was always alone
as are all men and women though they may pretend
to share the cultures they were born to
they walk solitary, hold no hand, catch
no eye but their own, in a mirror, silver
reflections to the contrary, we finally stand
          alone, if we stand at all.
Of all the men, of all the women, kings
queens or knaves, most never awakened.
I alone remain. As do you, if you are wise,
if you have the eyes to see, the wind to hear.

❥

We waken to the colors of these stones
the surge of this earth rising about us,
come to feel the separateness of all that
is not part of this rising, this high singing

o, how the land sings in its own solitude!

v

I, He said, am the song
the darkness and the light.
I came, and since then, there
has been sadness and death,
but not without hope, not without
that thin line that connects your eyes
to distant stars

vi

The wind rises now and dust skirrs by
the sandstone bluffs. A man may read
his destiny there: my father, mother—
my children and theirs, friends that move
past the barriers, touch my hands—

a flash of eyes like summer lightning over
the cap rocks and we know who we are
the land solitary in its greatness.
        we, purified, by that belonging.

Village Store

—Fort Sumner, 1936

I remember especially
the smell of kerosene
and apples . . . . stacks

of open boxes, neat rows of cans
tomatoes, peaches. "Hell, son,
I've known cowpunchers to save

for a month, come to town
and blow it all on canned peaches
evaporated milk and peppermint candy."

My mother saying, "A Carnation Baby,
that's what you were. I sent your
pictures in when they had all those

ads, but they didn't use them." General
Custer (remember him?) and all the cereal
I had to eat to earn his dying picture

with gold arrowhead stamps to prove I
ate my oats and was loyal to his command
though I loathe that brand (and him) to

this day, remembering the darker corners
of that store, the dust, the pickle barrels
those old men look up when I come in, always.

Revista

Now in these years when looking back
becomes blurred, uncertain, the days
too much like the nights, faces,
always reminding of another, thus
dismissed in their own certainties
because of a chance resemblance
to someone long dead, or lost.

—buoys on a still sea. Gullcries
haunt my head and still I long
for the sea fall that will announce
my coming home, my sailing in

—this windy mesa, no sea at all,
yet this waving grass, even the stubble
catches at my heart with the old
longing. How far is the home the heart
needs, how long the night's dawn
that awaits the coming of light.

Behind me, the moon rises.

Keith Wilson is a native New Mexican poet and short story writer. Graduated United States Naval Academy (B.S.) and the University of New Mexico (M.A., a.b.d.). Late Lieutenant, USN, combat veteran Korean War. Presidential Unit Citation, Korean Service Medal (4 Battle Stars), United Nations Service Medal.

Keith Wilson is Professor Emeritus in English at NMSU and has taught at several other universities. He has been Distinguished Visiting Writer at both Bowling Green, Ohio and at The United States Naval Academy, Annapolis, Maryland. His awards have included the National Endowment for the Arts Creative Writing Fellowship, The DH Lawrence Fellowship. The Senior Fulbright-Hays Fellowship (to Romania). Mr. Wilson has received The Governor's Award (NM) for Excellence in the Arts, The Premio Frontereza from the Border Book Festival for Lifetime Achievement, and is listed in the El Paso Writers Hall of Fame. He lives in Las Cruces with his wife Heloise.

Keith is a member of The Rio Grande Institute. Consultant to Coordinating Council for Literary Magazines (CCLM) 1972-74. Consultant for National Endowment for the Arts to Voice of America, 1975. Master Poet for The New Mexico Poetry-in-Schools Program. and pioneered Poetry in the Schools throughout New Mexico and Arizona.

Publisher's Note

PENNYWHISTLE PRESS CELEBRATES THE MILLENNIUM!

Established in 1986 the Press has grown, maintaining a lively conversation between the authors it has published and their readers as it hopes to continue relating to and with the poets, writers, critics, reviewers and readers of the future.

The Press has expanded its outreach and its books are distributed by Small Press Distribution of Emeryville, California and various other distributors and wholesalers.

The publication of **Bosque Redondo: The Enchanted Grove** by *Keith Wilson,* features another noteworthy poet whose distinguished voice reaches out to all. The concurrent publication of **Blood Trail** by *Florence McGinn* marks the 31st title in its Poetry series.

Pennywhistle's latest collection of distinguished and important poetry underlines the commitment the Press has made to share a wide range of voices, presented in a responsible manner to a public seriously interested in good work and an expansion of the landscape of poetry.

The Press currently offers the following titles in its Chapbook Series:

ρ

The Blue Series

Sublunary

Jorge H, -Aigla's writing goes to the heart of experience with clarity, illuminating truth as perceived by him. Taking his cues from the dark side of life, *Aigla* reaches out with caring insight..

32 pages $6.00, ISBN 0-938631-07-1

Full Turn

Sarah Blake's book exposes the sacred territory of domestic blood connections, of love and family–demonstrating how ordinary life has a tendency to trap and bind. *Blake* roots herself in the present and struggles with ghosts of the past, convincingly adept at being both here and there at once.

32 pages $6.00, ISBN 0-938631-05-5

Further Sightings & Conversations

Jerome Rothenberg has an overriding preoccupation with seeing. His work comes from a need for concentrated visionary representation. Shaman and High Priest of language, he sings as he explores and blesses the world.

32 pages $6.00, ISBN 0-938631-03-9

The Fields

Richard Silberg's work is spare and complicated and speaks to the process of personal discovery. His brilliant resolutions bring one home.

32 pages $6.00, ISBN 0-938631-05-5

Who is Alice?

Phyllis Stowell's preoccupation with the need for a common language between the sexes generates a passionately argued sequence of poems about silence.

32 pages $6.00, ISBN 0-938631-04-7

The Sum Complexities of the Humble Field

Viola Weinberg offers a poetry of the sensual that can be tasted and touched. At the same time, she presents her world with discipline and mathematical precision.

32 pages $6.00, ISBN 0-938631-06-3

The Red Series

No Golden Gate for Us

Francisco X. Alarcon's poems give simultaneous voice to the pain and humor of the desperado who has seen and felt too much and to the quiet understanding that comes with wisdom.

32 pages $6.00, ISBN 0-938631-16-0

Tesuque Poems

Victor di Suvero embraces a world grounded in arroyos and trees, lightning storms and streams. Complicated and thought-provoking, his poetry celebrates survival while praising the phenomena of existence.

32 pages $6.00, ISBN 0-938631-17-9

Hardwired for Love

Judyth Hill takes her readers on a lyrical roller coaster ride through ancient past toward a luminous future. Her essential message is direct, and her laughter, sensuality, intelligence and exuberance infuses her work with love, spiritual awareness and aesthetic discipline.

32 pages $6.00, ISBN 0-938631-13-6

The Width of a Vibrato
Edith A. Jenkins writes a poetry of affirmation that begins with awareness
of loss and is dwelt upon until the poet is able to transmute that loss
into affirmation.
32 pages $6.00, ISBN 0-938631-10-1

Portal
Joyce Jenkins poetry offers readers a rare combination of playfulness spoken with
wisdom–showing a complex nature devoid of bitterness.
32 pages $6.00, ISBN 0-938631-18-7

Falling Short of Heaven
Susan Lummis' work is the quintessence of a high strung, highly sensitive and
wildly intelligent woman's attempt to get along in this big, bad world. Her poetry
is written with a theatrical feel that makes it seem lived in.
32 pages $6.00, ISBN 0-938631-12-8

ρ

The Green Series

Where you've Seen Her
Grace Bauer has earned her reputation for a clear and incisive use of language.
Ms. Bauer illuminates her subject matter with an honesty all too rare in
today's world.
32 pages $6.00, ISBN 0-938631-11-X

Decoy's Desire
Kerry Shawn Keys' appreciation of the natural beauty of his world–specifically
that lush hillside in Perry Co., Pennsylvania–surfaces throughout this collection.
32 pages $6.00, ISBN 0-938631-14-4

What Makes a Woman Beautiful
Joan Logghe shares a voice as ancient and wise as time. With gleaming syntax
honed to perfection, *Ms. Logghe's* women–and men–live their everyday realities
and how "beauty" abides and sustains.
32 pages $6.00, ISBN 0-938631-15-2

Chaos Comics
Jack Marshall's work is sensual and intense; his supple, possibilities of perception
with a philosophy that is breathtaking in its audacity and scope.
32 pages $6.00, ISBN 0-938631-25-X

Between Landscapes
Wai-Lim Yip has created a magical, musical scale that enchants, soothes and lulls, rises and falls, as it simultaneously plunges us into the beauty and power of the terrible and sublime cycles of nature.

32 pages $6.00, ISBN 0-938631-24-1

Sextet One
The first anthology in Pennywhistle's new series. This volume presents the work of six separate and distinct poets with each presentation containing an introduction by a noted critic or poet, a photo of the author and a collection of the poet's most recent work–a wonderful way to bring six new friends into one's life! This volume presents *Kim Addonizio, Tom Fitzsimmons, Harry Lawton, Annamaria Napolitano, Doren Robbins and Ruth Stone, with introductions by Dorianne Laux, Victor di Suvero, Maurya Simon, Pierre Saint-Amand, Philip Levine and Rebecca Seiferle.*

226 pages $17.50, ISBN 0-938631-27-6

In the paperback full volume Poetry Series it offers it's latest publications as stated above.

Bosque Redondo
Is a moving collection of poems whose theme is the evocative power of memory. In the hands of the poet memory becomes the catharsis that opens up the world of childhood, a space the poet must revisit. Noted voice of the Post Beat era, *Keith Wilson,* friend of *Charles Olson, Sid Corman, Robert Duncan, Robert Creeley and Gary Snyder,* recognized the responsible voice of his time in New Mexico and in the West.

108 pages $12.00, ISBN 0-938631-28-4

Blood Trail
The cross-cultural currents that have enriched American writing in the later part of the 20th century continue to be part of the literary scene today. *Florence McGinn's* work continues that cross-cultural adventure. Her poetry, crafted with care for the detail of her Chinese heritage, reaches into our consciousness with current American scenes and with language that touches our hearts.

108 pages $12.00, ISBN 0-938631-34-9

naked Heart

This collection of *Victor di Suvero's* as poetry is a compendium of poems which dance between the wise old street experiences of San Francisco to the delicate and sensual places we learn to honor through love and time. This selection makes the case for love exciting, erotic, evocative and thoughtful...all at the same *time. Poet James Broughton says that, "di Suvero is valiant to take the risk of disrobing his heart—it's the only way to be a genuine poet."* And poet and Nuyorican Cafe founder, *Bob Holman,* has this to say: *"When you listen to the beat of di Suvero's collection, naked Heart, you will hear yourself falling in love with poetry."*

80 pages $12.00, ISBN 0-938631-28-4

Hooplas!

Is a collection of festive tributes to friends and intimates of the author, who salutes their talents and personalities with song, fanfare and wit. These odes for odd occasions are offered in praise of friendship, in memory of merriment, and in awe of love.The poet died in 1999 best left this special tribute to his many friends.

93 pages $8.95, ISBN 0-938631-02-0

ρ

In the Anthology Series it offers the following:
¡Saludos!

¡Saludos! Poemas de Neuvo Mexico is the first bilingual anthology of the poetry of New Mexico. Sixty six fine Native American, Hispanic and Anglo poets share their experience of the Land of Enchantment with clear and heartfelt poems that sing! Poets represented in this strong and unique collection include *Miriam Sagan, Jim Sage, Leo Romero, Charles Bell, Greg Glazner, Peggy Pond Church, Luci Tapahonso and Joy Harjo,* among others.

290 pages $15.00, ISBN 0-938631-33-0

Voces del Rincon/Voices from the Corner

A collection of the poetic personae of *Michael Sutin* addressing issues pertinent to life lived in the corners of the New Mexico landscape crossed by the network of the highways of today.

180 pages $15.00, ISBN 0-938631-33-0

Ordering Information
Call your order to 505-982-0066,
or fax it to 505-982-8116
or write to 930 Baca St., Suite 12, Santa Fe, New Mexico 87501